STEPHEN FOULKES considers that there are four things guaranteed to make a fool of a man – wine, women, sailing boats and horses. Since he has been intimately involved with all four, he reckons that he doesn't actually stand much of a chance. He retired as a sergeant in 1996 after 31 years' service with the police force, 20 years of which were with the Mounted Section in Bristol. In 1998 he published a history of Bristol's police horses to mark the centenary of the unit. He was also a police diver from 1969-1976. To add song to his list of intimates, on his retirement he developed his semi-professional singing career into a full-time occupation. He was subsequently employed as a bass-baritone soloist by choral societies across the country, including a 20-year spell as soloist for Bath Choral Society's annual Christmas performances of Handel's Messiah in Bath Abbey. He was a lay-clerk with Bristol Cathedral Choir from 1976-1986, and vicar-choral with Wells Cathedral Choir from 2002-2009. In a rare fit of lucidity, he joined the Somerset Registration Service as a Ceremony Officer Registrar in 2012.

ANDREW PREWETT studied Fine Art at Maidenhead Art College before entering the commercial world. In a long and successful career, he has worked for advertising agencies in Reading and London, producing adverts, logos, stationery and posters for many commercial products including Airfix kits and other children's toys and books. He later joined the BBC where he assisted in marketing and designing record sleeves. Later he became Creative Head of Department for a major record company, and worked on some of the world's leading artists releases. He then formed his own company, creating record and CD packs which influenced the industry world-wide, developing and using skills in 3D packaging. Subsequently he joined an international printing company, where his creative drawing, painting and sculpting helped further expand the group into multi-media areas including tobacco, pharmaceutical and communication products. His designs and illustrative influence became global, and he has a well-respected name connected with some of the most iconic creations in the world of packaging, music, and illustration.

Currently his fun-filled book, *100 Ways To Use A Walking Frame* has proved to be a great success, whilst other book illustrations are on his drawing board.

Dedication

For my wife Louise, who was determined to get me back to work, and discovered the perfect occupation to entice me back to the workplace. I'd be lost without her.

Stephen Foulkes

"I Do.... Don't I?"

Illustrated by Andrew Prewett

AUSTIN MACAULEY
PUBLISHERS LTD.

A CIP catalogue record for this title is available from the British Library.

ISBN 9781786298881 (Paperback)
ISBN 9781786298898 (Hardback)
ISBN 9781786298904 (eBook)
www.austinmacauley.com

First Published (2017)
Austin Macauley Publishers Ltd.
25 Canada Square
Canary Wharf
London
E14 5LQ

Acknowledgments

My thanks go to the following people:

Andrew Prewett, my illustrator, whose work, in my opinion, largely gives the book any merit it may deserve;

Genevieve Branch, Somerset Registration Manager, for reading the final draft, and in spite of that, allowing me to go to print;

Tricia Roche, Valerie Whaley, Fay Rogers, Joyce Lewis, and Vivienne Durrant (Auntie Viv) for bravely agreeing to proof-read early drafts;

all my colleagues in the Somerset Registration Service, especially those in East Somerset (Shepton Mallet and Yeovil) for being so supportive and friendly since I joined, which is possibly one of the best things I have ever done; other than getting married, of course;

and my wife Louise, who has patiently put up with my preoccupation with this project during the last few months. It was, of course, entirely her idea that I join the Registration Service in the first place, so it's all her own fault.

I do....   don't I?

FOREWORD

Since finishing this book, I began to wonder where it belonged. Ok, ok – I can hear you shouting, "In the bin!" – but before it reaches that receptacle, I wondered where it would reside if it ever reached the shelves of a bookshop or library.

A little while ago, I entered one of the well-known bookshops in the High Street to see if I could answer this question. I walked slowly between the shelves, noting the headings over each section which identified the general areas of interest – Fiction, Non-Fiction, History, Crime, etc. – to see whether my book had a natural home.

Yes, all right – 'Crime' is very funny but no court could convict, so forget it; and 'Horror' – don't even go there. Where else? 'Fiction' wouldn't do, because the stories are mostly true, although I have embellished one or two; 'Non-Fiction' would be too general a term; 'Humour' might be too generous; and 'Local Interest' too limiting. 'Fantasy'? I wouldn't be so cynical. 'Erotica'? No comment. I really couldn't find a place on the shelves to which anyone entering the shop could immediately go in order to find books of similar content to this.

In the end I decided that if it ever made the shelves of a bookshop, I would have to be content with either 'Local Interest', 'Humour', or even the dreaded 'Miscellaneous'. You may know of bookshops with more specific categories –

maybe 'Marriage' or 'Relationships' – but I was defeated in my search.

Of course, if it were down to the book's illustrations alone, the category would be easy. It would sit happily on the 'Humour' shelves, and even be at home amongst 'Fine Art'!

I very rarely have brainwaves, but I am still patting myself on the back for the moment when I thought of asking my cousin Andrew Prewett to provide the illustrations.

Andrew and I live at either end of the M4 corridor, and although we have always got on well together, we very rarely met. This changed in recent years, when I visited him more frequently at his home in order to see my 102-year-old Auntie Hilda, his mother. I had always known that Andrew's business was as a commercial artist, but only became more aware of his talent during my recent visits.

I believe that if my little book has any merit, it lies within its illustrations, and I am very grateful to Andrew for agreeing to take on the job. It has been a treat to work with him on this project, and to enjoy – and benefit from – the fruits of his labours.

I hope you enjoy them too.

INTRODUCTION

I half awoke and grunted as I turned over. Someone was moving and muttering nearby but I did my best to ignore it. I have never been at my best first thing in the morning, so to avoid having to engage my brain I pretended to be asleep. The muttering became louder, and was distinctly audible to me, but still I lay motionless and unresponsive.

Louise my wife (for it was she) gave a final exclamation of exasperation and left the bedroom. Minutes later I heard the front door slam and I could turn over and doze again uninterrupted. Bliss.

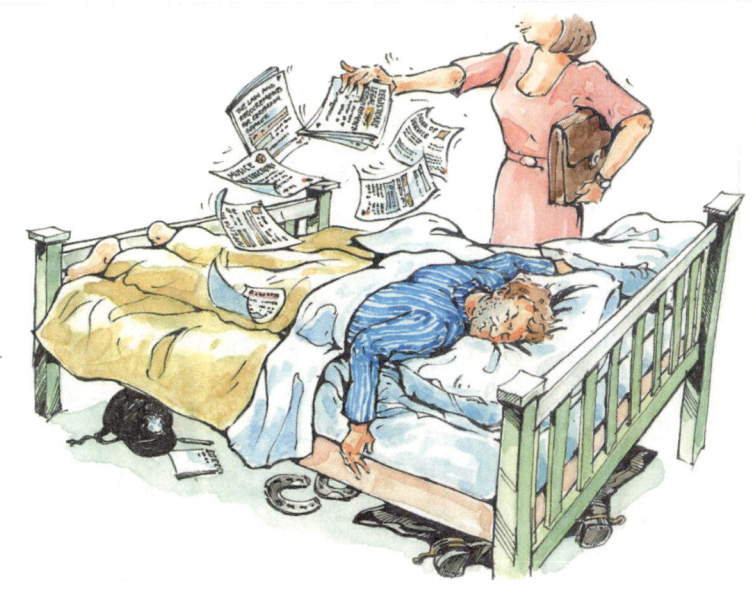

Since retiring from my career as a police officer I tended to luxuriate in lie-ins. I reasoned that I had done my turn at the coal face, getting out of bed at the crack of dawn, often in freezing weather, and making my way through deserted streets trying – mostly unsuccessfully – to pretend that I was ready for whatever the day would bring. That efficient state would generally not occur for another two hours at least, but I always did my best. So now I made the most of my freedom in the mornings, and I suppose I was inclined to overdo it, much to Louise's irritation.

Anyway, when she returned home that evening from her teaching, she surprised me with a bald statement.

"I want you to marry someone," she said.

I stared at her uncomprehendingly. Had she had enough of me being what I laughingly called a professional layabout, and did she want me out of her life? I couldn't really believe that was the case... so what did she mean then?

Louise continued: "I've been on the phone to Auntie Viv, and she's given me an idea. I want you to get a job, and there is one you might make a reasonable success of." (I was slightly affronted by her lack of confidence in my general abilities – even if it was justified – but I let it pass.) "You should become a registrar, and then I might not need to be the only one out of bed in the morning."

My mind raced (well, pondered) over the possibilities of what she was saying. I quickly discarded the idea of being a Medical Registrar. Not even in my sometimes inflated ideas of what I could achieve had *that* possibility occurred to me. Then I linked her first statement to her second, and realised she meant the recording sort of registrar – Births, Marriages, and Deaths, commonly called Hatch, Match, and Despatch.

"You'd be perfect for it," said Louise. "You have experience of dealing with people, and experience of performing in front of a crowd." That's true, I thought. After my police career I had been a professional singer, so those pieces of the jigsaw fitted quite neatly. Together with the undeniable fact that we needed to inflate the family budget, it seemed like an idea worth pursuing.

With more prompting from Louise, I found myself investigating the pages of the Internet to find out about the job and what, exactly, it entailed. My timing, it seemed, was spot on. After a few false starts I checked the Somerset County Council's web page and discovered that they were advertising for "Ceremony Officers", or registrars who specialised in the marriage aspect of registering.

I looked down the list of qualifications, and it dawned on me that I was able to comply with most of them. Okay, I was a little hazy about Spreadsheets and my academic qualifications (such as they were) needed to be massaged slightly, but other than that, it appeared that I was able to match the minimum criteria being sought.

I downloaded the application forms and carefully filled them in. I did what I thought most people do in these circumstances - I accentuated the positives and minimised (almost to the point of eradication) the negatives.

Finally I laid down my pen and read it through. I quite enjoyed doing that. Until then I hadn't realised that I was quite so perfect. How could they refuse me? I was obviously a paragon of virtue and efficiency, and they would be beating a path to my door begging me to take the job. I glowed with self-satisfaction, which only lasted as long as it took Louise to read it. She knows me so well.

"That's crap," she said. (She is not one to beat about the bush.) "I thought you were serious about wanting this job." She took her teacher's red pen and struck through 90% of my paean of praise, and made me start again.

Eventually I completed it to her satisfaction, and I had to admit that the application looked much more business-like. I now appeared to be an ordinary guy with the necessary skills for the job, instead of some kind of demigod superman condescending to consider employment with the County should they be so lucky. I put the application into an envelope and posted it off, hoping for the best.

Two weeks later I was invited for an interview. The last time I had put myself through a job interview had been nearly forty years before, and I imagined that the process had moved on a little in the intervening period. In the event I found the audition to be thorough but fair. It included "performing" a ceremony, legibly filling in a Register entry, completing a section of Spreadsheet (I was convinced I had made a mess of that) and answering pertinent questions from the county's registration managers. While it wasn't a picnic in the park – who does enjoy these things – I felt I had negotiated the day with reasonable success and headed home with optimism.

Well, I was lucky. Several days later I received a call from one of the managers to say that I had been accepted. I joined the Somerset County Council's Registration Service as a Ceremony Officer and so began a career which has taken me across the region to meet people on a lovely day in their lives and marry them in attractive venues all over the county.

Perhaps best of all, since most weddings begin during the afternoon, I was still able to enjoy my ritual lie-ins and ignore, with a little more self-righteousness, Louise's morning mutterings!

CHAPTER ONE

REGISTRARS

Following Louise's determination to rouse me in the morning, which resulted in my headlong entry back into the world of work, I quickly settled into the routine. I realised that it suited me very well. After all, I told myself, I'm meeting people on a happy day, and in beautiful locations – what's not to like? And another element which aided my transition back to regular employment was the pleasure of working with the people who were my new colleagues.

A registrar is an official keeper of records made in a Register, and this includes the recording of Births, Marriages, and Deaths. In my experience registrars are intelligent people who enjoy meeting the public and, with tact, extracting from them information which is required by law, of the happy or sad occasions in their lives.

Being mostly part-time, it was found that help was required to keep abreast of the number of civil marriages performed in the county, so it was decided to employ registrars who would only be used for the purpose of conducting and recording marriages. These registrars would be known as Ceremony Officers, and I was inducted into this select group in February 2012.

(In some other registration areas, Ceremony Officers are known as Casual Registration Officers. This conjures up, to me, a slightly laid-back informally dressed official, leaning against the desk, cigarette hanging from the corner of his mouth, saying to a couple, "So, you wanna get married, eh?" I think I prefer our title.)

The technical aspects of registration in Somerset are very efficiently managed by two people, one known as the County Registrar and the other the County Superintendent Registrar. Other registration personnel are nominated as their deputies. Hence my title, if I was recording a wedding, would be Deputy Registrar, or if I was conducting a ceremony, Deputy Superintendent Registrar.

In the police service, to achieve the rank of Superintendent is a lofty ambition to which I never aspired, so now to be able to style myself "Deputy Superintendent Registrar for the County of Somerset" seemed rather grand! I revelled in the novel dignity of a title 29 letters long. However, I soon realised my humble place in the great scheme of things, as I was actually on the lowest level of a vast pyramid, the apex of which disappeared into the clouds and ended with the Council's Chief Executive Officer.

I loved the work from the start. I enjoy the physical act of writing, and the discipline of completing entries legibly into the Marriage Register and on the Certificates of Marriage. As a former professional singer, I was completely comfortable standing in front of people to perform, and my voice still retained a resonance which carried in the largest venues.

Because of the nature of our work, the response from the public is overwhelmingly that of approval. That being the case, it was a surprise to me that my very first ceremony (which I attended as an observer) resulted in a complaint being made about us. The venue was the little Dovecote in Kilver

Court, and my colleague Ian Coombes was writing (completing the entry in the Register and marriage certificate) while Lin Handley conducted the ceremony.

It was a very cold day and snow was lying all around. Lin and I wore our dark overcoats, and Ian had decided, in view of the conditions, to wear his expensive red anorak which offered him the best protection. It was freezing in the Dovecote, and he had some problem keeping his fingers warm enough to write. He managed however, and was later photographed presenting the certificate to the happy couple.

Two weeks later I heard that a complaint had been made about (a) three registrars in attendance at the event – "almost more registrars there than guests" was the comment made – and (b) Ian's mode of dress.

The complaints were quickly addressed. The couple thought they had to pay for three registrars, when all I did was stand around and watch. They were soon advised that no, my attendance was free and was only part of my learning process. Ian's expensive red anorak was criticised as being inappropriate, and was probably highlighted by the fact that he appeared in one of the wedding photographs (which perhaps fortunately rarely happens). It was pointed out that the day was very cold and he needed to keep warm in the rather exposed venue. The complaints were withdrawn, but it was ironic that they occurred at my very first ceremony.

Incidentally, the marriage certificate, which is presented by the registrar at the conclusion of the ceremony, is sometimes given to the bride with the explanation that, traditionally, the document is her property. The reason is historical. In the past, brides may have married a sailor or soldier who was obliged to spend long months or years abroad, and left alone at home she would have needed the documentary evidence that she was, indeed, married.

In practice, these days the registrar will comment that the bride doesn't have any pockets in her "wonderful wedding dress" and will use that as a reason to present the certificate to both bride and groom.

When we enter the Registration Service as recruits, we are teamed with a mentor, an experienced registrar who shows us the ropes and guides us towards a good standard as Ceremony Officers. This includes instruction on all the legal issues involved, how to proceed with interviews, conduct ceremonies, fill in all the important legal documents, and tackle RON (Registration Online), which is a computer record of all ceremonies completed and entered in Registers nationally.

It is a proud day when, after a few weeks of training, you are presented with a pen full of registration ink, and let loose on an unsuspecting public. It's like being given your wings.

Registration ink is not like ordinary ink. It is made up of a special formula designed to remain readable for ever. If the world crumbled to dust, you could still read words written in registration ink. Sometimes at the signing of the Register, a bride or groom (or their witnesses) would produce their own expensive fountain pens with a proud flourish, only to be told that they couldn't be used because the ink was wrong.

Before a ceremony can proceed on the day of a wedding, the couple have to be interviewed to confirm that their personal details, which may have been declared several months beforehand, had not changed during the intervening period. When we interview the bride and groom, we follow a series of questions to confirm the accuracy of their details on the day of the ceremony, after which they can be entered into the Register.

The questions include details about their full name, age, condition (single, divorced, widowed etc.), occupation, address, father's details, and how their signature looks (for transcribing onto the certificate). I have the questions written down in my file to make sure I don't miss anything, but more confident colleagues just follow the headings over the details on the Certificate For Marriage.

My colleague Jeremy de Quidt had already completed a full year successfully conducting ceremonies, and was now progressing to the task of completing the legal documents. He declined to keep a copy of the pre-ceremony questions, preferring instead to take his cue from the Certificate For Marriage.

"And what is your condition?"

When we ask grooms and brides about their marital status ('condition') we say, "Have you ever been through any form of marriage or civil partnership before, in this or any other country?" They respond either, "No," meaning that they are single, or, "Yes," meaning they are divorced or widowed.

On this occasion Jeremy was questioning a bride, using the headings on the Certificate.

"What is the full name you are using today?"

The bride gave her full name.

"What is your age today?"

The bride gave her age.

"And what is your condition?"

The bride gasped, coloured up, and said, "Well, I'm not pregnant, if that's what you mean!"

Jeremy, equally embarrassed said, "No, no I mean have you ever been through any form of marriage?"

I believe he may be thinking about using a crib sheet after all!

There are occasions when a registrar from outside the county arrives to conduct a ceremony at one of our venues. This happens when the registrar is a friend or relation of either bride or groom, and has been asked by them to officiate. There is no objection to this happening, and the respective Registration authorities give their approval.

Somerset takes the view, however, that since the county is responsible for the ceremony, the home registrar (who is also required to attend) will sign the Register as Superintendent Registrar. Although visiting registrars should be advised of this, sometimes they are not, which can result in some embarrassment, which happened in this case.

My colleague Bobbie White and I met the visiting registrar Hilary (not her real name) at Pennard House, the venue for the ceremony. When we arrived, Hilary was striding around importantly, taking charge of the event. She had already briefed the groom and his best man about what was expected of them, and was now busily organising the readers and the photographer.

I half-sensed that we might have a bit of a problem with her, but set about preparing the certificate. As instructed, I wrote Bobbie's name down as the conducting Superintendent Registrar. Hilary immediately spotted this (she must have been on the lookout for it) and said, "No – you've got that wrong. That's where my name should be." She smiled smugly at me, anticipating that I would apologise before making a "spoil" and preparing another certificate.

But when I laid my pen down to explain the county policy to her, Hilary was most aggrieved. "My friends want my name on the document," she complained. "That's why I'm here!"

Bobbie said, "Well, you will be conducting their ceremony. Why don't you ask if you can also be a witness, then you can sign the Register and appear on their certificate?" It seemed an eminently satisfactory solution to me, but Hilary was having none of it. "My name should go down as Superintendent Registrar!" she complained. "Can you phone your SR and get permission?"

We knew that the county policy would not be changed just like that, so we refused. "Well then, phone GRO (General Record Office) and ask them! This isn't right!" Again we refused and again suggested she sign as a witness. She turned away, irritated by our stance.

Hilary knew we wouldn't be moved, so she decided to make the best of it and sign as a witness as we had suggested. However she had come intending to sign as registrar and she was obviously indignant that she couldn't do so. She perceived it as a slight and the refusal was very much resented. Thereafter she conducted a ceremony which, to me, lacked certain niceties (like inviting the witnesses to the front when the vows were recited; Hilary just let them stay in their places, a few rows back) but was efficient enough.

We exchanged a couple of pleasantries after the ceremony, but doubtless she went back to her home county complaining of her treatment and trying to get the policy changed. As far as I know, the policy remains the same, so I guess her efforts were unsuccessful.

It was unfortunate that the situation developed as it did, but I have to say that I believe none of our registrars would have reacted in the way Hilary did. If the situation had been reversed, we would have accepted it with good grace as befitting a guest in another registration area.

There are many potential hazards for Ceremony Officers to face as they enter a marriage room to conduct a ceremony. Mostly these come from the principals or guests, and have to be dealt with as you go along.

Among such hazards can be noisy guests, alcohol in the marriage room (not permitted), overwhelmed children, Best Men who believe they are the life-and-soul-of-the-party, music controllers who ignore your frantic requests to 'PLEASE TURN THE VOLUME DOWN', ring-bearing dogs who respond to the dictates of nature in the middle of the aisle, or birds which add their particular voice at the most critical part of the ceremony. In this latter respect, I am thinking of the peacocks at Hornsbury Mill, near Chard.

Upstaged

It is one of our most attractive and popular venues, and often ceremonies are held in the gazebo next to the lake, near the peacock's roosts. Occasionally the birds take umbrage at the invasion of their space by gaudily-dressed humans, and choose the time of the ceremony to give raucous voice to their objections. They also take the opportunity to demonstrate to everybody how *proper* plumage should look. I know many wedding photographs have been enhanced by these attractive gatecrashers.

Incidentally, it was while at Hornsbury Mill that I encountered another sort of hazard, and I had to take advantage of the first aid skills of Jane, the Mill's manager. While thumbing through the papers of the wedding file I somehow managed to give myself a painful paper cut on my right forefinger, and I started to bleed like a stuck pig. I was about to write in the Register and complete the marriage certificate, and I guessed that the bride and groom would not appreciate my blood splashing all over their documents.

I held up my injured digit pathetically to show Jane, hoping for a bit of sympathy, and thankfully she took charge and did an effective nursing job on me, washing and bandaging my finger tightly enough to stem the flow. I was able to continue without the fear of making the certificate look like some sort of grisly exhibit at the trial of an axe murderer.

Young children are sometimes overwhelmed by an adult occasion which they find difficult to understand, and they can become noisily tearful as a result. This is another hazard which may need the attention of the registrar. The strident yells of infants sometimes requires a decision to be made on the occasions when no adult takes charge by removing the upset child from the area.

The presence of children may be very important at the ceremony, because they are related to the bride or groom, or are being used as flower girls or pageboys. However, when decibel levels begin to interfere with the comfort of the couple or other guests, the Ceremony Officer has to consider whether to ask the bride and groom if they are content to continue amid the cacophony, or whether they would like the source of the noise removed.

Sometimes the upset child is the son or daughter of the couple, understandably objecting to being separated from its parents. A simple solution then is to allow the child to be held by mum or dad and be a close part of the ceremony.

The presentation of the rings can provide another hazard. The best man is usually required to bring the rings forward at the appropriate time in the ceremony, but sometimes the task is delegated to a child. The rings are often tied by ribbon to a small cushion to prevent them from falling to the floor, but this arrangement can present its own problems. It is amazing how often the pretty bow which secures the rings turns into the most fiendish knot when being untied in front of a roomful of people.

The bride, groom and I are left standing by helplessly while the ring bearer grapples frantically with the problem, and sometimes the only solution is to cut the ribbon with a pair of scissors which will hopefully be produced from a guest's handbag. Having witnessed this pantomime many times, I always advise against the use of ribbons and cushions, preferring instead the more traditional best man's waistcoat pocket.

As your experience grows, you learn to handle these and other hazards with humour and hopefully with your dignity intact.

On a visit to The Centurion Hotel for a ceremony, however, one of my female colleagues had a little more to deal with than is usually the case. The incident did nothing for her dignity but did provide the assembled company with an unexpected moment of levity. This colleague, I ought to add, is always very dignified and efficient, and luckily also possesses a keen sense of humour. Halfway through the ceremony, her skirt – for no apparent reason – suddenly descended around her ankles to show the entire room a nice pair of Bridget Jones.

She couldn't immediately retrieve the situation because both her hands were engaged in holding her script. Quickly she put her file down on the signing table and grabbed at the offending article of clothing which she hauled up to recover her modesty.

Her dignity however had been dealt a mortal blow, as everybody (after an initial gasp of astonishment) burst out laughing. But my colleague is a true professional, and once the mirth had subsided, she commented that fortunately nobody had been quick enough to take a photograph of her predicament, so she would happily deny everything!

My own source of embarrassment had nothing to do with the misbehaviour of clothing. Fortunately for the many guests before whom I have had to stand, my trousers have so far remained securely in place. But the following episode caused me similar angst.

So many wedding ceremonies come and go during the course of a year, that Ceremony Officers often have a myriad of names swirling around in their heads at any one time, and the trick is to make sure you apply the right names to the right ceremonies. Failure to do so can result in acute embarrassment, as you can imagine. It happened to me soon after I joined the Registration Service, and it taught me a lesson I haven't forgotten.

"Who's Emma?"

I was due to conduct a ceremony in Yeovil, which was part of a series of three weddings in one day. I had prepared all three scripts in one sitting the night before. (That's my excuse, and I'm sticking with it.)

The groom and bride in Yeovil were called John and Nicola, and I started the wedding confidently with my usual introductions, followed by the little "giving away" ceremony, when the bride's father agrees to hand over responsibility for his daughter to her new husband.

Then I said – addressing the roomful of guests – "Ladies and gentlemen, you know far better than me that John and Emma have found in each other happiness, fulfilment and love." I tailed off as everybody burst out laughing. I was puzzled for a moment until the bride leaned forward and said, "I'm not Emma, I'm Nicola!" I looked down at my script, and sure enough, I had printed the name Emma who was the bride at an earlier ceremony.

Acutely embarrassed, I said lamely, "Oh yes I do apologise, Nicola!" Then to cover my embarrassment I leaned toward John and said, "Now let's get this straight. John, do you know anyone called Emma?" John said (fortunately) "No!" which brought another gale of laughter from the room. I hope my red face had paled a little by the time we reached the main vows, when I managed to get all the names correct.

I apologised to the couple again after the ceremony, but thankfully they both thought it was a great laugh, and the story will probably be retold many times when the subject of their wedding comes up.

On another occasion I was filling in the Register on a table decorated with two small sweet trees. One was made up of liquorice Allsorts and the other consisted of Maltesers and small mints. A few feet in front of me some young bridesmaids were eyeing up the tempting display, and I could see they couldn't wait to get their hands on it. A couple of the mints had fallen onto the table from the tree, so to wind up the girls I made a performance of picking one up and popping it into my mouth. However the bridesmaids had more entertainment than I had bargained for as I realised that the sweets were actually made of polystyrene. I couldn't help making a face as I was forced to eject the "sweet" into my hand, which brought forth some smothered hilarity among the girls!

One of the most important parts of a wedding file is a document called the Certificate For Marriage. There is one each for the bride and groom, and they are commonly known as "the blues" because they are usually printed on blue paper. The documents, issued by the Registration Office at which the couple has given notice of their intention to wed, are required at the ceremony to confirm that they are legally entitled to marry. On the day of the wedding, the Deputy Superintendent Registrar and Deputy Registrar will both sign the Register to the effect that the wedding had taken place "by certificate before me".

Before one ceremony I had occasion to text one of my female colleagues, whom I was meeting at the venue, to tell her that I 'had the blues', meaning, of course, that I was in possession of the Certificates For Marriage and that the ceremony could proceed. As luck would have it, Louise spotted my text and unsurprisingly put a different interpretation on the comment. Her eyebrows only descended to their normal position when I explained the innocent reason for the apparently intimate communication.

The blues caused me further embarrassment one windy day at Wick Farm, one of our wedding venues near Bath. I was interviewing the bride while she was still seated in her bridal car outside the building, when a gust of wind snatched the Certificate For Marriage from my hand and blew it away towards a nearby field where it flitted madly about, obviously intending never to return. As I've said, ceremonies cannot proceed without the document, so I set off in immediate pursuit, leaving the bride and her bridesmaids watching in some amazement as their registrar galloped about the field trying to recapture the piece of paper.

Luckily for me, the pesky thing became trapped against a wall where, with some relief, I was able to swoop down and retrieve it. I returned with it to the bride's car and, somewhat breathlessly, resumed her interview against a backdrop of giggling bridesmaids. This was yet another occasion when my dignity became a luxury which had to be put to one side. Good job I'm used to it.

CHAPTER TWO
THE VOWS

"I Do!"

In the view of many people, these two little words, a mere three letters, seem to provide the very heart of a wedding ceremony. The words appear in the Catholic wedding service but not in "The Form of Solemnisation of Matrimony" provided in the Anglican Communion's incomparable Book of Common Prayer, when both bride and groom respond to the question "Wilt thou take N to be your lawful wedded wife/husband?" with the words "I Will." And similarly nowhere do the words appear as an obligatory part of the civil marriage ceremony.

The vows we are required to ask couples to repeat are the rather dry-sounding "Declaration of Freedom" vows and the "Contractual" vows, both of which are the only legally-required parts of the Civil Ceremony of Marriage, although we also make sure that no-one knows of any legal objection to the marriage, and advise that the marriage room is properly approved. The Declaration is a public announcement by the person involved that they are permitted to marry without any legal impediment. There are three alternative forms of wording, the simplest being to answer "I Am" to the question "Are you free lawfully……?"

The Contractual vows, again with three alternatives, require the groom and bride to publicly announce in turn that "I, N, take you N, to be my wedded wife/husband." Whereupon the details could be entered into the Register, and the deed was done.

However, in view of the happy, romantic, and often well-attended nature of civil wedding ceremonies, we Ceremony Officers surround the legal vows with other appropriate words which, we hope, will make for an enjoyable occasion for all concerned. Sometimes this will include a form of words which require the answer "I Do" which some brides feel have to be part of their ceremony, although they are, as stated, not a legal requirement. Often there are readings of poetry or prose which use the words, so it would seem appropriate to also include them during the ceremony.

My own marriage script does not require the couple to utter the words "I Do" (unless specifically requested) but it was the response I expected from someone else closely involved in the ceremony. Early in the proceedings I would turn to the bride's father and say "Do you, bride's father, give your daughter's hand in marriage to the groom?" and the response (if you were lucky) would be "I Do." Sometimes they said "Yes" or "Hmmmmm. I suppose so" or "Which one?" or even "I can't wait to get rid of her!" or some other witticism. Then dad would sit down next to his wife to be either uncomfortable with, or impervious to, her cross stare.

"Thanks, dad, you can let go now... dad?"

I've even had a father, in response to the question, launch into what appeared to be the start of a lengthy speech. "Yes I do, and it's been a privilege and a pleasure to bring my lovely daughter up, and deliver her to this important moment in her life. I know she'll be very happy with Ian, and as soon as I met him..."

"Yes, thank you, sir, you may now return to your seat!"

One sunny day in Spring I set off with my colleague Val Whaley to travel down to a famous venue in Cricket St Thomas. The ceremony was to take place in the Manor House there, and it may be remembered as the house in the TV series "To The Manor Born" starring Peter Bowles and Penelope Keith.

(I should add here that two registrars are always required at wedding ceremonies; one to conduct the ceremony – the Superintendent Registrar – and one to complete the entry in the Register and fill in the couple's marriage certificate. On this occasion I was conducting.)

We drove down a long avenue towards the building, and admired the honey-coloured stone and well-tended gardens. The groom welcomed us, and as usual we interviewed him, and later his bride, to ensure that accurate personal details could be entered into the Register and on their marriage certificate. The groom Peter was English and his bride, Saskia, was Polish but with a flawless command of the English language.

However her father, Stanislaw, whom she wanted to give her away during the ceremony, had not a word of English.

So using his daughter's services as translator, I explained to him what was required.

"When I ask you" pause for translation "do you give your daughter's hand" pause for translation "in marriage to the groom" pause for translation "you respond with the words I Do" pause for translation "and then you can sit down" pause for translation.

Stanislaw looked at me uncertainly, and then said in a thick accent "Oi duh." I said, "Well if you like, you can say it in Polish." The bride translated, and Stanislaw said "No, no – I will say it in English." He went off to a corner of the room muttering "Oi duh... Oi Dooo... Oi Do... I Do..." Saskia seemed satisfied so I said, "Well, I think he's got that."

The time of the ceremony approached, so I entered the elegant room which was full of wedding guests. I noted that Val was ready, having prepared the certificate and Register. I called the assembly to order, gave my usual chat about mobile phones and photographs, and at the signal that Saskia was ready, said, "Ladies and Gentlemen, please stand for the entrance of the bride!"

Everyone stood up, and Saskia entered on her father's right arm. They processed along the short aisle, with Stanislaw swelling proudly as he noted the guests admiring glances. They approached the table where I was waiting and stopped in front of me. Peter and Saskia grinned broadly at each other, and Stanislaw stared fixedly at me, waiting for his moment.

"Ladies and Gentlemen, may I take this opportunity to welcome you to Cricket St Thomas on this very special day for Peter and Saskia." I was aware of Stanislaw's gaze. "My name is Stephen Foulkes…" and I went on to introduce myself and Val.

Then I asked the bride and groom to confirm their names, which they did. I half-noticed Stanislaw start slightly as they spoke, but I continued with my opening remarks – "this place has been duly sanctioned according to the law of this country." Stanislaw began to shuffle slightly, but I continued "...if anyone knows of any lawful impediment why they should not be joined in matrimony, you should declare it now."

Unexpectedly, and in a loud, proud and stentorian voice, Stanislaw said, "I DO!"

Well, I'm used to coughing and odd noises at this point, but Stanislaw's interpolation brought the house down. Saskia turned to her father in alarm and said "Nie teraz ojciec!" (Not now father!) Everyone else was doubled up in laughter. Poor Stanislaw coloured up when he realised what had happened, but order was soon restored.

When afterwards, I pointedly turned to him and asked the question "Do you give your daughter's hand…..." he replied, only slightly less loudly than before, "I do," which received a generous round of applause and a beaming smile from Saskia. As the ceremony proceeded he took his seat with some relief.

Whereas the Declaration and Contractual vows have to be recited accurately, any other vow included in the ceremony could be tailored according to the couple's wishes, and thus personalised by them for their wedding. Hence I could ask the groom and bride "Do you take N to be your wife/husband, and do you promise to....?" with the expected wedding response of "I do." There was no objection to this being included if desired.

We are not permitted to use any of the cadences from the Book of Common Prayer, so any reference to phrases such as "to have and to hold, from this day forward, for better or worse, till death us do part" was forbidden.

The ring vows, however, allowed open season on the terminology, provided there was no reference to the Anglican vows ("With this ring I thee wed....."). The ring vows offered by the Registration Service are a bit bland, but if you aren't concerned to compose your own, they are perfectly acceptable.

As with the legal vows, the Ceremony Officer would recite the lines in short sections for the couple to repeat. Occasionally the bride and groom were so nervous that the short sections had to be *very* short, and sometimes even reduced to single words in order to coax it from them.

I didn't, as a rule, have any problems with personalised ring vows. More often than not, the couple would read them to each other from properly printed cards or (very rarely) recite them from memory.

Occasionally however, I was requested to "feed" the lines to a nervous bride and groom, which sometimes resulted in intimate words, which were fine when expressed by the loving couple, sounding rather comical when recited by the straight-faced Registrar -

Registrar: "I will love you forever..."

Groom: "I will love you forever..."

Registrar: "I look forward to cuddling you..."

Groom: "I look forward to cuddling you..."

Registrar: "And will kiss your tiny toes..."

Groom: "And will kiss your tiny toes..."

Okay, that didn't actually happen, but you get my gist. I have had to feed lines which were not really suitable, among them being the line "I take you to be my luvver." But usually we managed to persuade couples to read the more intimate vows, and I always take a copy along to ceremonies in case they hadn't prepared anything.

I recall a ceremony in the Council Chamber of the Mendip Registration Office soon after we had moved there. The couple – and indeed the whole party - were what I call the "salt of the earth" type and were inclined to wise-cracking and general hilarity throughout, although in the main, I managed to keep a lid on it.

However, I nearly lost it when the groom tried to place the bride's ring on her finger, and after several unsuccessful attempts at pushing and pulling, said in a loud voice, "Yer – you're getting fat, ain't yer?"

I've heard some comments at this point of the ceremony when the ring declines to fit snugly, but this remark was by far the most ungallant. I said to him, "I'd keep quiet if I were you." Luckily for the groom, the bride had a similar sense of humour and screeched raucously at the joke.

A colleague recently told me of other comments innocently uttered by the couple when attempting to fit the ring, which the assembled guests took to mean something completely different. When the groom found he was unable to slide the ring onto his bride's finger, she said, helpfully, "Lick it." The groom innocently replied, "Later." It was several minutes before the ceremony could continue.

In our multicultural society we often have to read out names during the vows which appear to be almost unpronounceable in our native tongue. The names of Eastern

41

Europeans seem to be very difficult for us, with Polish names being particularly awkward. Consider, for example, Krzysztof Grzegorz Jarogniew, or Malgorzata Mieczyslawa Przemko.

When faced with such names, the Ceremony Officer, after consultation, will always make an attempt at correct pronunciation, often to the huge amusement of the couple and their guests. Fortunately the important moment comes when the names are recited by the couple themselves, after which the Register entry can be (carefully) filled in.

I remember one ceremony in Kilver Court, near Shepton Mallet, where the groom was Sri Lankan, and his name was Warnakulasuriya Patabendige Amarasuriya.

My colleague Bobbie White was conducting the ceremony (thank goodness) but I had problems of my own, in trying to fit all the names in the little box in the Register and certificate while keeping it legible.

"Can you repeat that again, please?"

That would be problematic enough, but the groom's father was also present, and his name was Chaturanga Shasinramuthali Amarasuriya which also had to be entered in the box under the appropriate heading. I'm glad I had my ink-pot handy because the ink in my pen ran out twice while writing the names. I don't think I've ever written such tiny letters, but somehow I managed to fit it all in.

I suppose I should have been grateful that their respective occupations (also required to be noted in the Register and certificate) weren't Telecommunications Engineering Assistant Operations Under-Manager, or something similar.

The groom actually had a nickname (I think it was Pat – how sensible) which Bobbie was able to use throughout the ceremony, but when it came to the Declaration and Contractual vows the full names had to be recited. Bobbie had practised for days beforehand to get the pronunciation correct, and recited the name apparently effortlessly, much to the admiration of all present. Her efforts received a well-deserved round of applause!

On another occasion my colleague Maria Pitman and I went to Holbrook House near Wincanton for a ceremony where the bride was Korean. Maria was conducting the ceremony and I was filling in the Register and completing the marriage certificate. The bride's names weren't unmanageable this time, but she had asked for the Declaration and Contractual vows to be translated and recited in her native tongue.

We always like to accommodate a couple's wishes with regard to their ceremony if it were possible, so Maria had agreed beforehand to do so, once the vows had first been recited in English in order that I could understand them and begin filling in the Register. Maria managed the task very well, much to everyone's admiration, and the bride was pleased and happy, which always makes the extra effort worthwhile.

Sometimes we officiate at ceremonies which celebrate a past wedding, perhaps a special anniversary of the event or a renewal of vows. One Canadian couple had hoped to marry in an English castle, but their arrangements for the date of the ceremony had been disrupted by the legal requirements of residency. Their many guests had already organised their holidays to coincide with the marriage of their friends, and the couple did not want to disappoint them all, so they hit on a scheme to marry secretly in Canada and then go ahead with a form of marriage in England which, for their guests, would be the real thing.

The couple had been told that we couldn't marry them again in a legal wedding ceremony, but that our "Eternity Ceremony" (basically a renewal of commitment in marriage) could be adapted to make it appear that it was a proper wedding. I was to conduct the ceremony, and when I arrived at the venue (a mock castle not far from Bath) the first thing I wanted to know was who, on the day, would be aware that the couple were already married. The groom told me: "No-one else – only you and my wife and I."

I groaned inwardly. I now had to conduct a ceremony which was, for the guests, a marriage, and to all intents and purposes the real thing. With the best will in the world, our Eternity Ceremony cannot be mistaken for an actual marriage, and I pointed out that when the Eternity Ceremony Certificate was signed by the couple's witnesses, they would see that it wasn't a marriage certificate. The groom said: "Don't worry about that - I'm sure they won't notice!"

In the event, that is what happened. I massaged the vows enough to make them – for a foreign assembly – sound sufficiently genuine while not venturing into actual Declaration and Contractual vows territory.

When it came to signing the certificate, I think the witnesses were so dazzled by its official look (it is resplendent with coats of arms and immaculate copperplate writing) they didn't notice the heading which clearly said "Certificate of Eternity" and the line which stated "Neither the Ceremony nor this record or any other document relating to the Ceremony has any legal status."

I pointed out where the witnesses should sign the document, and when they had done so, I hurriedly sealed it into an envelope and presented it, with some relief, to the bride and groom.

If I had earlier felt a little guilty about the subterfuge which was being played, I soon overcame that when I witnessed the happiness of the couple and all their guests after the ceremony. The couple had paid for an Eternity Ceremony and that was what they received. I hope they managed to keep the secret from their friends for the remainder of their holidays and beyond and perhaps for the rest of their lives!

CHAPTER THREE
WEDDING MUSIC

It's not only the civil wedding vows or readings at ceremonies which are subject to the rule that dictates that there should be no religious content. The ban extends also to the music allowed at civil ceremonies. Some people are surprised at this, and wonder why it is so. I believe that the ban is historical, and has been imposed on civil marriages by the Church itself.

Long ago, the Roman Catholic Church, and subsequently the Protestant and non-conformist offshoots, together with other religious foundations, had an almost total monopoly on the act of marriage. If you wanted to marry (and of course this socially-acceptable condition was massively encouraged by the religious authorities) you were obliged to carry out the service of matrimony through the good, and sometimes expensive, offices of the Church or other religious establishment.

The preparation for, and act of matrimony was carefully controlled, and only comparatively recently has the vice-like grip been relaxed. The Marriage Act of 1836 allowed for non-religious marriage ceremonies to take place in Registration Offices, and ever since, the State has increased its influence in the matrimonial stakes. A recent calculation estimated that 70% of all marriages now take place under the auspices of the State rather than the Church.

"Dear Sir, I take up my pen in some heat..."

The 1836 Act had many opponents, and prominent among them was the imposing figure of Henry Phillpotts, the Bishop of Exeter. You can almost hear the gnashing of teeth when he stated, in a letter to The Times, that the Act was "...a disgrace to British legislation... not solemnised by the church, marriage may be celebrated without entering a consecrated building and will be equally valid whether it takes place in the House of God or in the house of a registering clerk, one of the lowest functionaries of the State." Ouch.

The State also started keeping national statistics round about the middle of the 19th century. Non-Anglican couples were obliged to have a civil official present to document their marriages, as it seems that they weren't to be trusted to record the marriages themselves.

Unsurprisingly, the Church was not content to share its marriage liturgy with the State-run version, and it was agreed that its time-honoured words, based (in the English Protestant tradition) on Thomas Cranmer's timeless and incomparable marriage service in the 1549 Book of Common Prayer, would not be permitted to be used in civil ceremonies. This has been the case ever since.

The religious ban for civil ceremonies includes any of the vows, readings, and the music performed at the ceremony. I would guess that the Church hoped to continue to attract couples for whom the traditional words and music were important, and with which the State-run version could not, at the time, compete.

Nowadays the vast wealth of popular music available can and does provide music for wedding ceremonies, and has probably reduced the influence of the Church in this sphere at least.

We are instructed as Ceremony Officers to be aware of this general non-religious rule, and although it does not normally present problems, just occasionally we are obliged to indicate what is not permitted actually on the day of a ceremony. Couples are advised when giving notice about the rule, and readings and music are normally vetted at this stage to eliminate any inclusion of religious content. Sometimes however, music can slip through the net, and I have on occasion asked those responsible for the wedding music not to play certain pieces.

I have to say that, as a singer who has performed, appreciated and enjoyed a vast and wonderful range of religious music, it grieves me to ask, for example, that extracts from Handel's "Messiah" be turned off at a ceremony. There can be no reciting of Psalms 67 or 128 (both common at Church weddings) and no songs containing religious sentiments, superb pieces of music though they may be. Mozart's beautiful "Laudate Dominum" had to be scratched from one ceremony (imagine!) and The Lord's Prayer, of which there are many great musical arrangements, cannot be allowed.

Incidentally, my own legal wedding took place on a beach in New Zealand (permitted in that country). A few months later we enjoyed a Wedding Blessing in Wells Cathedral, with a full panoply of choir (Louise's operatic friends and my then colleagues the professional singing-men of the Cathedral, known as the vicars-choral) accompanied by the organ, singing their hearts out to wonderful music by Mozart, Parry, and the Cathedral's assistant organist, David Bednall. I mention this to demonstrate that once the legal obligations of a ceremony are completed, the limitations imposed are removed, and couples can give free range to their imaginations and dreams. Once the marriage certificate is in their possession, they can have ceremonies jumping out of aeroplanes or as part of a dive to the ocean floor, or they can engage a full choir and orchestra to perform "Messiah", should they so wish.

I was recently asked by the leader of a string quartet performing at a ceremony about a piece which had been requested by the couple, and which was actually included by name in their printed Order of Ceremony. The piece was Bach's "Sheep May Safely Graze" from Cantata 208 and the leader (who knew of the religious ban) wondered whether it was allowed.

Bach's music is mostly religious, but he did write a number of secular cantatas, and I knew that this was one of them, also being known as the Hunting Cantata. To be honest, even if it had been a sacred cantata, I would probably have still allowed it on this occasion as it was to be an instrumental version (no words) and would not be known to be irrevocably tied to a religious text, unlike (for example) the well-known "Jesu Joy of Man's Desiring" from Cantata 147.

Most of the music played at the ceremonies in which I have been involved have been from the pop music field, and usually have a special meaning for the couple ("our song"). Occasionally live music, in the form of piano, piano and voice, guitar or harp and voice, or string quartet, would be part of the event, which I always thought preferable to any recorded music. One of the most popular pieces (in the classical field at least) is Pachabel's Canon, and many a bride has processed down the aisle to its familiar strains.

On one occasion I was discussing possible music choices with a bride, and she knew enough about the Canon to sing a few notes of it, without really knowing much about the piece. She frowned and searched around in her memory for the title. Then her face cleared. "I know!" she said. "It's the music from that computer firm – you know – Packard Bell and Canon!"

The traditional processional and recessional music for weddings – Wagner's Bridal Chorus from Lohengrin ("Here Comes The Bride") and Mendelssohn's Wedding March – are rarely, if ever, heard at civil ceremonies. I imagine that the pieces, arranged for organ, are so closely associated with weddings in churches with their superior acoustic, that they are not often considered as alternatives when performed through sometimes tinny-sounding music-players in smaller secular buildings. The pop music choice is almost always the preferred option in such circumstances, perhaps wisely so. The overwhelming sentiment of most of these songs relate to the emotion of love, so it is hardly surprising that this is the case.

I once conducted a wedding at Pennard House when a full 30-voice mixed choir provided the music. They entertained the guests with a variety of secular numbers while waiting for the bride's entrance, but as it happened, she was late (now there's a thing) and consequently they had run out of pieces to sing.

I was at the back of the wedding area preparing to interview the bride, when I heard the choir launch into a distinctly religious song – a Negro Spiritual, I believe it was, and a fine arrangement of it too, by the sound of it. They had selected it on the spur of the moment as one of the few numbers they knew from heart.

I could have rushed down the aisle and demanded that their conductor stop the performance forthwith, as I suppose I was entitled to do, but that would have left a very sour impression on everybody, not least the choir. So I ignored it and told myself that as the ceremony hadn't actually started, it was okay (it isn't). And anyway, the choir was very good, and I sneakily quite enjoyed the performance.

Fortunately the bride arrived during the Spiritual, so the choir's next piece was the previously agreed processional music, which they launched into with admirable gusto. I said earlier that I always prefer live music, so I'm glad, in the end, that I didn't discourage them!

CHAPTER FOUR
THE VENUES

One of the nicest aspects of a Ceremony Officer's job is that he or she has to travel all over their area and sometimes county-wide to visit approved venues to officiate at weddings. The venues could be hotels, castles, manors, mansions, barns, town halls, farms, caves, pavilions, gazebos or even pergolas (of which more later). They all had one thing in common, and that was they had received a visit from the County Superintendent Registrar to confirm their suitability for wedding ceremonies.

The criteria ranged from Health and Safety issues (for example the number of guests the venue could safely accommodate), to ease of access, (which was required in case the groom's current wife needed to point out a legal impediment), and other aspects of suitability for the event. Once authorised, they are duly licenced as 'Approved Premises' and are able to host legal wedding ceremonies. Most of the venues are highly attractive, made even more so by their efforts to decorate their marriage rooms for the occasion.

We also had to attend weddings at churches. Not, of course, Anglican churches – they are the Established Church and run their own marriage services. In most circumstances all others needed the attendance of a registrar in order to perform a legal ceremony. The minister conducting is obliged, at some point in the service, to include the Declaration and Contractual vows in addition to any required by his or her own church. Then the Register can be filled in and signed by all parties including the officiating minister, the marriage certificate can be completed and presented, after which the registrar can depart. Job done.

The district in which I operate has its fair share of attractive, interesting, and downright unconventional venues which it is (normally) a pleasure to visit. The "responsible person", who helps arrange the venue's organisation of the marriage and attends to the registrars on their arrival, brings the groom and witnesses to us for interview and later escorts us to see the bride in her room or bridal car.

I suppose one of the more unusual venues in my area is Wookey Hole Caves. Three of these world-famous caverns are approved for wedding ceremonies, and couples for whom this is appealing come from all over the country to marry in the bowels of the earth.

The marriage cave is always spectacularly decorated with candles, and a signing table and registrar's table is provided together with a table lamp to illuminate the writing surface in what would otherwise be a very dim light. Sometimes when conducting I use my backlit iPad, which in the dimness is much easier to read than my usual script. We sometimes take umbrellas with us to the cave, because water dripping from the ceiling could otherwise make a mess of the Register entry or the marriage certificate.

One of my first ceremonies took place in Wookey Hole Caves. The venue attracts unusual and unconventional clients, and occasionally weddings have involved the participants dressing as Harry Potter characters or as prehistoric people. On this occasion the couple were members of a Witches Coven and they, and all their guests, dressed accordingly.

My colleague Tricia Roche was conducting the ceremony while I completed the entry in the Register and prepared the marriage certificate. We, the registrars, would normally depart the scene once the legal parts of the ceremony were finished, but as the guests blocked our exit, we moved to the back of the cave and stayed behind (in a completely unofficial capacity) to watch the proceedings.

When we had finished our ceremony, a man came forward dressed in black shirt and kilt and carrying a broomstick. I wondered for a brief moment whether we were to be treated to a flying exhibition, and I was quite disappointed when I realised that wasn't going to happen. He recited some words over the newly-married couple, who responded with words of their own.

Then with a flourish, the black-kilted man flung the broomstick down on the floor of the cave, and the couple immediately jumped over it – whereupon (according to their

Order) they were married. One for the book, I remember thinking at the time.

Unconventional though these and others like them were, the couple and their guests appreciated our involvement in the legal part of their ceremony, and were anxious to comply with our instructions and follow the rules.

Incidentally, until recently marriages were required to be conducted between the hours of 8am and 6pm. New legislation has repealed that requirement, making it possible for couples to be married at any hour of the day or night should they so desire. We Ceremony Officers are now all waiting to find out who will be the first to conduct a midnight ceremony in Wookey Hole Caves on Hallowe'en, which someone is sure to want before much longer.

Another memorable ceremony in the Caves involved a couple who each cited their occupation as "funambulist". This means, apparently, "an acrobat who performs on a tightrope or slack rope". To prove their credentials, a wire was strung high over the cave entrance, and both bride and groom, dressed in their wedding finery, climbed up and proceeded to the middle of the wire without mishap, where they waited for the registrar.

I felt a bit uneasy as I clambered up the ladder to join the couple balanced high over their guests. When I reached the platform, I very slowly and carefully moved step by step along to the middle of the high wire, trying not to look down, and readied myself to perform the ceremony.......no, not really, you may be relieved to hear. The couple's trick was performed for the benefit of the local TV cameras outside before they were later married inside the caves.

Another entertaining ceremony in the Caves involved the CBBC programme, "Marrying Mum And Dad". Youngsters plan a wedding for their parents, who have no idea about the plans, which typically include the theme, the venue and the outfits. The parents know they are getting married – just as well I imagine – but the children plan everything else.

On this occasion the venue was Wookey Hole Caves, and the theme was prehistory with the odd tyrannosaurus thrown in. Everyone dressed up accordingly, and I even spotted some convincing dinosaurs cavorting for the cameras. The couple were hugely enjoying the event masterminded by their children, while aware of the solemnity of the ceremony itself. A large bonfire (red, yellow, and orange ribbons fluttering up from a stack of wood) had been built in the cave, and the couple and their guests stood on one side of the "fire" while I conducted the ceremony from the other side.

I attempted to use my best Laurence Olivier voice during the ceremony, because I am aware that my speaking voice can sound a bit West Country at times – attractively so, I flatter myself – and for the recording I thought it might be better to temper it. I needn't have been concerned though. I was not seen at all when the programme was broadcast, and my only audible line was "You are now husband and wife!" which was delivered in a slightly-less-than-Olivien accent. All that make-up for nothing.

Often I left my area of East Somerset to help out in other parts of the county, and I always enjoy my excursions into beautiful parts of the countryside. One of my favourite trips is to Haselbury Mill near Crewkerne. It is a building which was erected over 10 years ago but was designed along the lines of a medieval Tithe Barn. I first visited the location when I was employed as bass soloist for the local choral society's performance of Verdi's Requiem, and I was hugely impressed with the building which was able to provide a lovely large space under the main roof as well as a "Belvedere" (large gazebo) for use when it was dry.

The only difficulty with this arrangement concerned the vagaries of the British weather. One couple had decided to use the Belvedere for their ceremony, and it was duly decorated for the event, with a hundred or so chairs placed in front of it for the guests. Then an hour before the ceremony was due to start, the clouds rolled across the sky and it began to drizzle with rain.

The groom reluctantly agreed that the whole party should retreat into the Barn, so the chairs were moved inside and the main hall prepared.

Then twenty minutes before the ceremony was due to begin, the clouds vanished and the sun came out, bathing the Belvedere in a glistening rosy glow. After a brief hesitation, the groom decided to return to Plan A. The very efficient Minnie, the responsible person, privately rolled her eyes heavenward and gave her orders. Frantic activity followed, with all hands carrying everything back outside. The Belvedere was reinstated as the venue, and all the chairs were back in place in the nick of time - where they were going to remain, said Minnie, even if a storm of biblical proportions intervened.

On another occasion we arrived early at one of our large venues, and we were able to observe the very hard-working staff carefully placing all the chairs throughout the length of the marriage room. The task was meticulously done, with great care being taken to ensure equal distances between the individual files and rows of chairs. When the job was completed, the result was an isometric marvel which was a wonder to behold. I was amused to note, however, that as soon as the chairs were all satisfactorily in place, another member of staff was dispatched to sweep the entire room from back to front. I didn't have the heart to suggest that, just perhaps, it might have been better to sweep the room *before* the chairs had been placed?

Another favourite destination is the town of Dunster, on the west Somerset coast. Dunster Castle itself is, unsurprisingly, an approved venue and I have conducted several weddings there. The town also boasts a Tithe Barn, and I remember driving down to the Barn in glorious weather to conduct a ceremony with a local registrar. I always expect the bride and groom to dress up appropriately in their finest clothes for their ceremony, and I am rarely disappointed.

On this occasion, however, the theme seemed to be "earthy", with the groom dressed in a casual jacket, corduroys, open-necked shirt and colourful waistcoat, and the bride in a light green wedding dress and wearing a crown of herbs and blooms on her head. On her back she wore a large pair of gossamer wings.

She was a very slight girl with an elfin-shaped face, and I wouldn't have been at all surprised if she had fluttered down the aisle to join her groom. Her bridesmaids were similarly adorned, and the "fairy" theme was continued in the decoration around the Tithe Barn, which provided a most agreeable atmosphere.

The lovely manor at Brympton d'Evercy, just outside Yeovil, is another venue which is always a delight to visit. The marriage room is set in a chapel-like building next to the main house, and it is invariably beautifully decorated for ceremonies with floral displays, both on the signing table and along the edges of the satisfyingly long aisle. It makes a very attractive pathway for the bride and her entourage as they enter.

Candles are placed around the room to enhance the atmosphere, including a line along the front of the signing table. As I prefer to stand in front of the table when conducting (unless by doing so I obstruct the view of a particularly fine floral decoration, when I would stand behind) I take care not to get too close to the candles in case I set fire to the tail of my suit. While doubtless entertaining for the guests, the sight of the registrar stripping off his coat, throwing it to the floor and stamping on it to extinguish the fire would not add much to the solemnity of the occasion.

The Town Halls at Glastonbury and Wells are also popular venues for wedding ceremonies, and each location is able to provide halls for over 100 guests, as well as attractive rooms for smaller numbers, and Mayor's Parlours for the very intimate ceremonies involving only the bride and groom and two witnesses.

The town of Glastonbury is a near neighbour of Worthy Farm, where every year the biggest music festival in Europe is held. This is known locally as 'The Pilton Pop Festival', but its proper title is the rather more grand, 'Glastonbury Festival of Contemporary Performing Arts'. As a result of its proximity, adherents of the alternative society are attracted to the town, and I conducted one ceremony in the Committee Room at the Town Hall, about the time of the Festival, where the bride and groom were dressed as flamboyantly as I've ever seen at a wedding. The groom wore a highly-coloured shirt and matching trousers, while the bride's dress was an extravagant mix of eye-popping hues which were undeniably and I imagine intentionally garish.

No-one would have been surprised if I'd worn my sunglasses for the ceremony, and on reflection I think the bride and groom would have approved, as I would have appeared quite 'cool' wearing them! The couple were at least true to their type and enjoyed the short ceremony which made them man and wife.

Mentioning Glastonbury Festival reminds me that two years ago Tricia Roche and I were preparing to marry a couple who intended to travel up to our Office from the Festival site, and then return as husband and wife to continue their enjoyment of the event. The ceremony was scheduled to take place at two o'clock in the afternoon, but when the time arrived there was still no sign of the bride and groom. We tried several times to contact them on the phone, without success.

Eventually, about 90 minutes after the ceremony had been due to take place, Tricia managed to make contact with them, and it appeared that the traffic had been so heavy around the area that the couple were unable to make any progress in our direction. They had therefore decided to give up and return to their tent on the site. Tricia made appropriate sympathetic noises and offered to rearrange the ceremony for later in the week, when travel would have become easier. The would-be bride's reply (in keeping with the famous atmosphere at the Festival) was so laid back, it was almost horizontal. She said, airily, "No, I don't think we'll bother." And as far as I know, they never did bother.

Another wedding in the Mayor's Parlour at Wells Town Hall was completely different from the flamboyance of the Glastonbury ceremony. I remember this one because the atmosphere would have been more appropriate at a funeral wake. The groom was ordinarily dressed in open-necked shirt and grey slacks, and the bride, though smart, could equally well have been dressed for shopping in the High Street. Both bride and groom appeared to be utterly miserable throughout the ceremony, in spite of my attempts at levity.

I can tell you that it is a bit disconcerting to be opposite two mildly distressed people on what is supposed to be a happy occasion for them. To my relief there was no hesitation when it came to repeating the vows, so I can only assume that they had either heard all my jokes before (quite likely) or that nervousness brought out that reaction in them.

Speaking of dressing up (or down) for weddings, I was recently involved in a ceremony at another unconventional venue in our area, the Haynes International Motor Museum at Sparkford. This spectacular establishment boasts hundreds of historic and vintage vehicles, all in top condition and glinting magnificently under the lights. Ceremonies take place in the American Hall where a variety of Stateside cars are displayed. Think "Bonnie and Clyde" without the machine-guns and you get the idea.

The couple and guests for this particular ceremony had decided to enlarge on the idea and they had come dressed in the fashion of the 1920s and 1930s, all Art Deco and Flapper. It made for an interesting scene. The men had dressed in light blue and cream three-piece suits and were wearing fedoras or flat saucer caps, while the ladies wore their chic straight dresses adorned with boa scarves and long necklaces, all topped off with cloche hats.

The music of George Gershwin completed the effect, and set against the backdrop of cars from the era, it made for a very glamorous event. The photographer was certainly spoiled for choice with his pictures, and was later no doubt able to present a spectacular portfolio to the couple.

I have enjoyed visiting every venue in the county for ceremonies, every one, that is, bar one. With my colleague Jan Lawford, I visited a newly-authorised building called Limpley House (name changed to protect the guilty) and as soon as we walked in we saw that no notices had been posted. These are normally required to be displayed prominently at venues, and indicate where the wedding is to be celebrated, together with a map, and the building's certificate of authorisation.

No-one met us on our arrival, and the location of the wedding was not immediately apparent. I knocked on an office door and the owner answered. I introduced myself, and asked where the ceremony was to take place. The owner indicated a nearby room which was full of heavy furniture including two small tables, one of which was laden with floral displays and small ornaments.

I said, "Have you forgotten to post your notices?" The owner responded, "What notices?" Although I was sure he would have known about them in view of the recent approval, I explained what was legally required. I ended by saying "…and a plan is required showing people how to get to the marriage room."

"Why?" he asked. "There's the front door, and there's the room. It doesn't need a map!" I refrained from saying that it was not obvious that it *was* a marriage room in view of its unpreparedness, merely observing that the notices were a legal requirement with which he must comply. "Well, I'm a solicitor – I know all about the law!" was his response.

He was about to return to his office but I asked him to move some of the furniture in the room to make a space in which to conduct the ceremony. He did so with minimum effort and bad grace, then disappeared back to his office. We interviewed the groom, who knew nothing of our contretemps with the owner. During the interview, Jan was forced to use an awkward low round table to complete the certificate and prepare the Register.

As the time of the ceremony approached, I knocked on the office door again to ask the owner to take us to see the bride, as we had no idea where in the building she was preparing. He took us to the bride's room which was some distance away on the first floor, then disappeared again while we interviewed her. Then, as usual, we left her to her final preparations and returned to the marriage room.

The time of the ceremony came... and went. No sign of the bride. I knocked on the office door (for a third time) and asked the owner to escort the bride to the marriage room. "Oh, do we have to do that?" he asked. I explained that it was usual for the owner or his agent to escort the bride at the appropriate time to the marriage room. She was, after all, a stranger in the house and might wander the corridors for ever seeking her lost groom (or words to that effect).

Eventually the bride entered the room and, negotiating the heavy furniture, arrived at her groom's side. The ceremony proceeded satisfactorily, with Jan nobly coping with the Register and certificate entries on the low table which was at a level with her knees.

Before we left the premises, Jan and I decided to have a word with the owner to confirm his responsibilities, as he seemed oblivious of them. I knocked on the office door, for the fourth time, and we underlined for him and his wife, who was also present, the legal and courteous responsibilities they had as host and hostess for the wedding.

The owner looked a bit chastened and reluctantly agreed with our comments, but we had taken on a new adversary in his wife, who gave the impression that it was all a bit beneath her, remonstrating that she had been told nothing about posting notices. I knew this was untrue, as our County Superintendent Registrar is highly efficient – I hope she is reading this...

I explained that part of our duty as registrars was to check that the legal requirements were being complied with, and unless they were met, and a room more suitably prepared for a ceremony, together with more co-operation on their part, we would be forced to report the matter to the County Registrar for her attention, especially with regard to the notices. Mrs Owner snorted and said, "Oh, it's all a bit petty, isn't it?"

Jan and I left determined to take the matter further, so I later prepared a report for the attention of the County Superintendent Registrar. I believe they received a visit from that august authority soon after, and although I haven't been back to the venue myself, I noticed recently that ceremonies are still being performed there, so I guess their service has been improved.

I am glad to say that this type of incident is very rare indeed, and we have received only the most courteous and professional attention from all the personnel at our other venues.

As you may be aware, civil ceremonies in this country have to be conducted under cover, although the definition is loosely applied. Hence pavilions, gazebos, summerhouses, and even sheds may qualify for the event.

We have a popular venue in Somerset where ceremonies take place in an open-sided converted cow-shed ("Summerhouse" said the responsible person, correcting me with only a hint of amusement). It is set attractively in the garden of the venue, and the Ceremony Officer can conduct most of the ceremony outside where the guests can participate, while the registrar sits in solitary splendour inside the shed... sorry, summerhouse.

"I moo…"

When the time came for vows to be exchanged, the bride and groom together with their witnesses, would step into the sh...summerhouse, perform their vows, then step out again for the rest of the ceremony.

Other venues around the area are suitable for these manoeuvres on a sunny day, including the very beautiful Dillington House near Chard, the Pavilion at Pennard House, and the Dovecote in Kilver Court Gardens. One *al fresco* location which I did not appreciate, however, was at an old Manor House near Yeovil, where a pergola in the garden of the house had been approved for ceremonies.

"Do you, Noah, take Raine to be your wife...?"

It is a large pergola, well-covered by colourful flora, and on a dry sunny day would certainly provide a very beautiful location for the ceremony. On the day I was there, however, the skies were grey and overcast, with rain threatened at any moment.

My colleague Steve Cooper, who was conducting the ceremony, offered to go inside the House but the couple wanted to remain in the pergola. As you know, pergolas provide only a few leaves as cover and as they are not particularly waterproof, we had to hope for the best. As a precaution I asked a guest to stand near me with a golf umbrella as I sat with the Register at a small table.

The timing was perfect, inevitably. As the bride and her entourage processed through the avenue of trees towards us, the heavens opened and I spent the rest of the ceremony crouched under the umbrella trying to keep the documents dry. I was only partially successful, and to this day that entry has several large splodges across it from the rain. I think in similar circumstances in future, I will listen to the vows *in situ* before retreating into the House to fill in the Register.

As far as I know, this is the only pergola in our area approved for ceremonies and I for one am glad about that. Perfect on a warm sunny day, but otherwise I prefer the comparative comfort of the great indoors.

CHAPTER FIVE
PHOTOGRAPHERS

I love photographers - no, really. They have a role to play at the ceremonies and as registrars we have to accommodate them and their particular needs.

Sorry if that sounds a bit tongue-in-cheek. Actually most of the photographers with whom I have had dealings are friendly professional people who are aware of the limitations imposed on them at a ceremony and will comply with our instructions. When this happens, I and my colleagues are prepared to agree to their requests for particular access or shots, within reason.

Perhaps I should explain what is and is not permitted in capturing the event on camera. Yes, I know it's the couple's day and they want it recorded, but not to the extent where every part is dictated by the camera. The importance of the ceremony is paramount, and its meaning should not be jeopardised or reduced by intrusive photographers.

The main rule, which is legally enforced, is that no photographs are taken of the Register while the couple are signing. The reason is that other people's personal details may be displayed on the same page, and Data Protection prohibits the copying of such details in any form. To alleviate this, we always take along a blank Register (or one is provided by the venue) plus an empty fountain pen with which the couple can pose for their pictures.

Incidentally, when presenting the empty pen to the couple for the photographs, I normally explain that the reason is to prevent them from writing rude messages in the blank register, and the light-hearted comment generally eases any tension the couple may have been feeling. In the past when full pens were used for this job, the temptation was for them to scrawl a romantic note on the page, but I have also seen drawings and comments (written by couples who obviously needed no relaxing) which would make a dockyard navvy blush. The empty pen at least forestalls this temptation.

The blank register and empty pen pose does not normally present a problem. But occasionally I have had to remonstrate with enthusiastic photographers for whom this arrangement is not satisfactory. One photographer explained to me that "immediacy is my medium" (no, I don't know what he meant either) hence he needed the actual signing. Others try to take photos from a distance, and while this may seem innocent enough, modern equipment can still include remarkably clear pictures of the Register entry.

Another trick is to try to take photos from below the table level, arguing that the Register cannot be seen. What they really wanted was to get close to the table and when no-one was looking, lift the camera for a picture of the actual signing. I have on occasion received black looks from photographers when I've prevented them from taking their low-level pictures. To forestall all this I, and my colleagues, maintain a strict "no photo" rule during the signing, as it is our duty to do.

Sometimes we are aware of a photographer trying to take pictures of the signing in spite of our instructions, and on these occasions I interpose myself between the Register and the camera. Several photographers across the county have very fine photos of my bottom, which even I must agree is not my best side.

Other restrictions are concerned with the disruptive, intrusive or distracting factors in photographing weddings. We really do try to accommodate most requests, but sometimes the cameras flashing, or continuous moving of the photographer, can be most distracting – especially if you are trying to concentrate on filling in the Register and certificate, when one error can mean a "spoil" and having to start again on a new certificate with the delay that incurs.

I remember one occasion at a Manor House near Taunton where the bride and groom were heavily involved with the media in a professional capacity – TV, radio and magazines. Consequently they both wanted every aspect of their nuptials recorded for posterity, both on video and in still photography.

I explained to them that in no circumstances could I permit the actual signing to be photographed – and when they heard the reason they readily agreed – but I was prepared to allow considerable leeway otherwise, provided my colleague who was filling in the documents was not disturbed.

Well, by the time I realised my mistake, it was too late. From the moment the bride set foot in the room, the photographers were omnipresent. I lost count of how many there were - possibly five or six, although they were all moving around so rapidly it was impossible to be sure. They stood between the couple and their guests to get shots, they put their cameras between the couple to get wedding ring shots, and one of them tried to get between me and the couple for a picture until I headed him off. Several times flash was used, and lenses were pushed into faces for close-ups. It was a nightmare for me.

The bride and groom seemed blissfully unaware of the photographic melee. I assume they must have lived their lives in the glare of such publicity, and it was probably all normal to them.

When the time came for the signing of the Register, I stood sternly by *daring* anyone to take a picture and my thunderous glare must have been effective, because they all stood meekly to one side, waiting for the blank Register. Then all hell broke loose again, as the desperation to take photographs dominated the closing moments of the ceremony. I swear I could see flashes behind my eyelids for hours afterwards.

The happy couple remained oblivious to the scrum, and posed, dare I say, professionally when asked. The main objective is the satisfaction of the couple with their ceremony, and on this occasion they obviously enjoyed all the attention. I filed the memory away, and hoped that I never had to experience anything like it again. Thankfully I never have.

There was one ceremony, however, where a single photographer caused me more embarrassment than the whole troop in Taunton. This was a lady (who will remain anonymous) who was obviously under the impression that she, and she alone, was in charge of the ceremony and was the most important person there, bar none. When she issued her instructions, she expected to be obeyed. I was conducting this particular ceremony and spoke amicably with her about not photographing the signing. I was lulled into a false sense of security.

The ceremony was in a local Dovecote, a pretty place but small. The guests were gathered outside, and I decided to conduct the ceremony mostly outside so they could all hear, then go inside for the Declaratory and Contractual vows. The photographer requested – or rather demanded – that the signing table be moved from its usual position in the Dovecote to a place nearer the door, and after speaking with my colleague Jan Lawford and the couple, I agreed to move it.

When the bride processed towards her groom, there was a moment when she had to retrace her steps so another picture could be taken. The photographer then asked me to stand in a particular spot so she could compose her photograph. By this time I had the impression that she thought she was in charge, so I refused and stood my ground.

The ceremony proceeded happily after that, until the bride and groom were seated at the table in the Dovecote with the blank register in front of them, ready for photographs. The photographer came in and peremptorily moved everyone around, seeking her picture. Fair enough. But then she demanded that Jan, who was busy completing the marriage certificates, move her table because the corner of it was getting into shot. We moved it a foot or two, which wasn't enough apparently, and as the certificates still had to be completed, we left it where it was. I could almost hear the photographer tut-tutting in irritation at our intransigence.

Once she had finished her work inside, she left the Dovecote and I followed her out to address the guests. I always allow friends and relations a moment to take any photos they wanted once the official photographer had finished.

I said: "Ladies and gentlemen, if you would like to take your photographs, now is the time." Then to my amazement, in front of all the guests, the photographer called out, "No it isn't!"

I gawped for a second, and then said, "Pardon?"

"There isn't room in the Dovecote for them," she said loudly. "And anyway, there isn't time!" She may have had a point about the lack of space which may have resulted in a bit of a scrum (but I was still prepared to allow it) and I suppose I could have stood there and argued with her in front of the assembly, but I knew it would have left a poor impression on everybody. Instead I said, "Ah. It seems the photographer says that we don't have the time – I'm sorry about that!" At least I put the blame for the refusal firmly at her door, but it left me feeling very cross with her attitude.

I tried, after the ceremony, to speak with her but she was busy with the couple and guests, organising them into groups ("You vill stand over there..."). I had to content myself with imagining what I would say to her, given the chance. While far less satisfactory, at least it meant I didn't appear in the local paper the following morning, under the headline "Registrar Slaps Photographer In Unprovoked Attack..."

Very uncharitably, I shall now refer to another incident with a photographer at the Dovecote, wishing it could have happened to the character just referred to. Sadly, it didn't. The Dovecote faces a narrow strip of grass where the guests usually assemble, and beyond that is a very attractive ornamental lake. The lake is several feet deep at this point - you're probably ahead of me, aren't you?

This particular photographer stationed himself between the two sets of guests with his back to the lake, taking his shots. As the Ceremony Officer announced the couple as husband and wife, the bride and groom turned to face their applauding guests. In his anxiety to get a good picture of the moment, the photographer took one step too many backwards, over-balanced, and with all his equipment strapped to him, fell with an almighty splash into the lake.

There was a concerted cry of alarm from everybody. However it can be said that the photographer (valuing his equipment more than his life) within a split second had hurled his cameras back onto the bank, before accepting assistance from the wedding guests to clamber back onto dry land himself.

The cry of alarm very quickly turned to restrained sniggers of amusement. He made a somewhat comical figure as he collected his strewn kit and then squelched wetly away to check on the damage, before returning with a dry camera for the signing photographs. Needless to say, my colleagues were sympathy personified.

Another uncomfortable incident involving a photographer took place at Wick Farm, near Farleigh Hungerford. The marriage room is an attractive stone barn, which is very popular as a wedding venue. It is usually decked out with floral displays and dozens of candles for the wedding ceremony.

The photographer generally stations herself by the wall behind the table prepared for the signing of the Register. There is a ledge along the wall on which candles are placed, making a glowing backdrop for the guests as bride and groom make their vows.

My colleague was halfway through the ceremony when she smelt something burning. She said, "I think I ought to stop the ceremony for a moment, because I'm sure something is on fire!"

Immediately there came a loud shriek from behind, as the photographer realised that, in leaning back to take a picture, she had trailed her head over a candle and ignited her hair. There was pandemonium for a few seconds as the photographer was chased around and cornered so that the fire in her hair could be extinguished. Fortunately no lasting damage was done or injury caused, so in due course the ceremony proceeded with the somewhat shaken photographer resuming her task perfumed with the acrid smell of burnt hair. It made a good story for the new husband and wife to relate as an incident in their marriage ceremony.

Some of these incidents may give you the impression of an "us and them" situation with ourselves and photographers, but that isn't really the case. As stated, the majority are very professional and accommodating, and we on our part are happy to help them get their photos, standing aside when appropriate.

There is a photographer in our area who, for the mock signing, insists on producing a large quill pen, possibly a foot long, which to me looks more comical than dignified, although the bride and groom always appear happy to pose with it.

On another occasion I produced an empty red-coloured pen for the mock signing. The photographer flung up his hands in horror. "Haven't you got a black or silver pen?" he said. "It will look better than that thing." My colleague produced another pen, but then I noticed that the themed colour for the wedding was red. The groom and his best man wore red ties, the bride had a red sash, and the bridesmaids' dresses were startlingly crimson. The colour red dominated the wedding room, so my red pen would probably have been lost in the background, anyway!

I had an impression, when I joined the Registration Service, that I, as Superintendent Registrar, would be asked to feature in lots of wedding photographs. This impression was reinforced after I had observed my first ceremony, when Ian Coombes (he of the red anorak) was asked to pose for a photograph when he presented the marriage certificate. However, in all the hundreds of ceremonies at which I have subsequently officiated, I have only once been asked to pose with a bride and groom.

This is, of course, as it should be. We are, after all, only the legal functionaries to whom people are obliged to come for a civil union, and the happy couple have far more important people in their lives with whom they would wish to be pictured for posterity. In addition, we often have to vacate the premises in some haste in order not to be late for the next ceremony, so we would invariably make for the exit as soon as the new husband and wife recessed back up the aisle.

However, whereas I have no problem with missing out on the photographs, I have occasionally cast an envious backward glance at the trays laden with glasses of champagne which are being prepared for the post-ceremony celebrations.

CHAPTER SIX
BRIDES, GROOMS, AND GUESTS

The most important people in any wedding ceremony are, of course, the bride and groom, followed closely by the witnesses and officiant. As a Ceremony Officer it is usually a delight to meet the principals in lovely surroundings on an important and happy day in their lives.

Sometimes as the weeks and months go by, with wedding after wedding, the ceremonies tend to blend and then fade in one's mind unless some funny or unusual incident occurs which makes it stand out and for better or worse (if I can use the expression), more memorable.

I should say that 96% of our customers are normal people engaged in the events of the ceremony, for all the right reasons. It may sound as if I am stating the obvious, but I feel obliged to underline the fact, because quite a few of the characters in this chapter are from the 4%, and I don't want to give the impression that we are always dealing with oddities.

The human condition is varied and diverse (thank goodness) and it takes all sorts to make up the world. We do encounter the occasional "bridezillas" who, probably due to nerves, make life a misery for all around them with their demands, orders and counter-orders, but fortunately such volatile characters are comparatively rare.

One of the first ceremonies I conducted was in the rather plain marriage room of the old Shepton Mallet Office. The groom was a slender lad of about 23, and his bride was a large lady about the same age. He was obviously very nervous, and bounced around from foot to foot as he awaited her entrance.

His bride entered the room, and paraded down the short aisle to take up her position by her groom's side. (I was reminded of the Joyce Grenfell song about a stately galleon sailing across the floor, but dismissed the thought.) She smiled at her groom but he stared fixedly at me, too nervous to relax and enjoy the occasion.

I proceeded with the ceremony, trying with my usual feeble gags to lighten his mood but without success. The couple gave me their full names, and we went on with the Declaration vows.

The groom continued staring at me as if his life depended on it, and I felt his bride was becoming a little irritated at his lack of communication with her.

Then came the Contractual vows which the groom had to recite first, and I said, "Turn and face each other, and repeat after me..." They did so, but then the groom instantly turned his head back to look at me, and his bride took hold of his chin and forcibly turned his head in her direction. "Look at me!" she muttered. He gave her a nervous grin, but when I began to feed him the lines, he looked at me again as if it would help his memory.

Once again the bride grabbed his chin, forcing him to look at her. He pulled his head away, apparently irritated, and actually recited one line directly at her. Sadly for him, when I gave him the last line he turned to look at me again. Before I knew it, she had lifted her left hand and given her groom a resounding slap in the face.

I would have fallen to the floor under such a blow, but in spite of appearances he was made of sterner stuff. He looked at her amazed and said, defiantly, "Don't you hit me!"

My first thought was that this could be the shortest marriage in the history of the world, but the assembled guests all fell about laughing, and I guessed this sort of behaviour was not uncommon among them. I laughed it off, and the ceremony proceeded without further incident. It may even have had the desired effect on the groom, because he relaxed visibly after the assault.

That wedding was between a slender man and rather rotund lady, but soon after this I officiated at another ceremony, again in the Registration Office, with a very corpulent groom and a stick-thin Thai bride. He was in his 50s and she gave her age as 32, but she looked much younger, as they often do. When I interviewed them beforehand, the groom explained to me that they planned to wed in a Buddhist ceremony in the bride's village in Thailand, but before that they wanted to undergo a marriage ceremony in the UK so that their union could be ratified here.

The Thai bride had a good command of English, but in circumstances where either bride or groom do not understand the language, an interpreter is required to translate the ceremony for the couple during their vows, and then to relay the responses in English to the registrar. The interpreter is subsequently required to sign as a witness in the Register.

This is also the case where either or both of the principals suffer from deafness, when a visual signing interpreter participates during the ceremony and then signs as a witness.

One of my many excursions into the rest of the county took me to Bridgwater Registration Office, and it was there that I had my only – so far – halt in a ceremony. Actually I stopped it twice, for different reasons. We are entitled to stop ceremonies if we think either party has been coerced or is under the influence of drink or drugs. (Any other illegality has normally been ironed out before it gets as far as the Ceremony Officer.) As you can imagine, you have to be pretty sure of your ground, as the repercussions can be very serious.

I had already interviewed the groom, who along with his best man, had a pretty earthy sense of humour. After the interview, he asked me "Can I say in my vows, 'I take you, wench'? You know, just for fun." I nearly split my sides laughing (not) and explained that the vows had to be recited correctly for the marriage to be legal.

I thought that I had negotiated the awkward part of the partnership until I met his bride. She was weeping with emotion and almost incoherent with nerves. She was what I later called "emotionally incontinent". Her demeanour was such that for a moment I thought she had indulged in a few too many pre-nuptial drinks, but there was no smell of alcohol, and her father assured me that she was a naturally highly-strung type inclined to react to any emotional stimulus. Well, that's just wonderful, I thought. Between her sobs, I managed to get the required information out of her and advised her how the ceremony would proceed.

When we were ready and she entered the marriage room, I could see that the situation hadn't improved. She clung for dear life onto her father's arm, weeping copiously, and eventually arrived at her groom's side. When we reached the moment at which she had to repeat the Declaration vows, I wondered whether she would ever get through them. Several moments later, I made a decision to offer her a halt.

I said, "If you don't feel able to continue, we can stop for a while so you have time to recover." She immediately grabbed my right arm and sobbed, "Oh no, oh no, please, please, let's go on!" So I continued with her vows which she managed to repeat a little more coherently. And just as I thought my problems were over, the best man (who was obviously a life-and-soul-of-the-party type) began making wise-cracks to the amusement of most of the assembled company.

I struggled on with the Contractual vows, and sure enough, instead of saying "wife" the groom said "wench." I stopped him and we went back over the vows which he then recited properly. Naturally the groom's humour brought forth more paroxysms of mirth from the guests, and the best man, not to be outdone, cracked another funny.

By this time I'd had enough and felt I had to regain control of the event. So I said sternly, "I am going to stop the ceremony now."

They all gaped at me.

I continued: "I would like to point out that this is an important moment, and a solemn ceremony of marriage. I want you all to settle down and behave with a little more decorum if I am to continue."

Perhaps my choice of words was ill-considered – I'm not sure they knew what the word "decorum" meant – but my general demeanour left them in no doubt that I was serious. They settled down, with the best man looking especially sheepish. I was able to continue, and I'm glad to say that the rest of the ceremony went without incident.

I tried to lighten the somewhat crestfallen mood, but in the end I was just happy to complete the proceedings and wave them off to enjoy the rest of their lives together. I have no doubt that the reception was a total riot.

The moment in the ceremony when we ask the assembled company whether they "know of any lawful impediment" why the couple should not be joined in marriage, has always had the potential for a little humour. I normally let the silent pause extend for a few seconds before saying to the bride and groom, "It's going jolly well, isn't it?" Colleagues occasionally say, "You've invited the right people!" or similar comments to help relax the couple.

More often than not, the moment is accompanied by a theatrical cough, or a loud scraping of chair legs on the floor, which is something we always expect and mostly ignore. I (and as far as I know, my colleagues in Somerset) have never, once the ceremony has commenced, encountered a serious objection to a marriage. Should such circumstances occur, and the objection seemed to be genuine, the Registrar would be obliged to stop the ceremony to investigate.

This type of incident is, of course, extremely rare, because any real objection would come to light much earlier in the process, and well before the ceremony itself. Should such a thing occur, it would entail a very uncomfortable time for everyone concerned, as the objector would be taken to a private room for the objection to be examined. It is insufficient to say, like the song, "It should have been me!" It would have to be a legal objection along the lines of knowing that the bride or groom were already legally married to someone else, and either produce documentary evidence to back up their claim, or be adamant that their objection was genuine.

Real evidence would result in the wedding being halted for further investigation. When such evidence was lacking, the Registrar would have to consider the circumstances, and the veracity of the objector, in order to decide whether or not to proceed. As I say, a very uncomfortable time for everybody, and I am very glad I have never actually had to deal with such an incident.

One of the interesting features of the job is noting, for the Register and certificate, the occupations of the couple and their respective fathers. I have already mentioned the "funambulists" which is an occupation which doesn't crop up very often. One groom I married in the Shepton Mallet Office gave his occupation as "Truffle Hunter". He was a country type of character, and insisted, before signing the Register, on making a speech about how happy he was, and thanking "the gods above"! I was slightly concerned that he would make other religious comments (which aren't permitted) but fortunately he decided to cut his oration short to continue with the signing.

Another couple in Glastonbury both gave their occupations as "author". I hadn't read anything they had written, but I do remember their names – his surname was Squirrell (pronounced "Squir-*rell"* he said) and her name was Fairladie. Both wonderful names. Sadly I heard later that the groom had died three months after his wedding, and I recalled that he had not looked well at the ceremony.

When we had moved, early in 2015, to our new offices in Shepton Mallet, one of my first grooms gave his occupation as "Sled Dog Driver". I thought at the time that you don't get many of those to the square mile in Shepton Mallet. It transpired that he normally lived in Norway, where I imagine his talents were put to more obvious use.

Similarly, and again in Shepton Mallet, I recently married a young Slovakian man who gave his occupation as "Figure Skater". Given the paucity of ice rinks in the area, I was pretty sure that men pursuing this type of career locally were very thin on the ground.

Not long ago I conducted a ceremony at Rook Lane Arts Centre, a former non-conformist chapel in Frome, where the bride and her attendants were covered in tattoos. Necks, arms and legs were vibrant with colourful scenes and complicated designs. The bride wore a low-cut dress displaying a generous cleavage, upon which was a large inverted v-shaped tattoo of an intricate pattern. I tried not to stare, but my eyes were drawn to the area in spite of myself. Well, I ask you – when a tattoo is applied in such an obvious place, isn't it there to be looked at and admired? I later noted the groom's occupation and was not surprised to see that it was listed as "Tattoo Artist".

Regretfully we are not allowed to use abbreviations in the Register or certificate, so "HGV Driver" has to become "Heavy Goods Vehicle Driver". That's a manageable occupation. Whenever the groom gives his occupation, or that of his father, as "IT Engineer and Lecturer" or "BT Investigator and Installer" my blood runs cold, wondering how I'm going to fit "Internet Technology Engineer and Lecturer" or "British Telecommunications Investigator and Installer" into the tiny boxed area provided.

Even that is preferable to 'Psychopathologist' or 'Psychophysicist' which sometimes crops up. I'm quite good at spelling, but in the stressful and time-limited situation of a ceremony, I need to carefully copy each letter, because a rush to complete the entry, or a moment's lack of concentration, can bring about a mistake which will result in a messy crossing-through in the Register, or worse, a complete "spoil" in the case of the certificate. Certificates have to be 100% correct, so any misspelling or misinformation means another has to be completed.

It is no wonder, therefore, that we *love* occupations such as "chef" or "nurse" and similarly, names like Mark Mud or Amy Tar, much more manageable than Warnakulasuriya Patabendige Amarasuriya, Chaturanga Shashinrahmuchali or indeed Krzysztof Grzegorz Jarogniew.

Speaking of names, I was officiating at a ceremony near Weston-super-Mare some time ago, partnering Denise Bigwood from the Bridgwater Registration Office who was conducting the ceremony. I hadn't studied the Certificate For Marriage very closely beforehand but noted that the couple were Chinese. When I came to interview, almost the first thing the bride said to me was, "Can you call me Ken?" I was somewhat surprised until I looked down at their Certificate, which listed the couple's personal details.

Her name was Wan-ken Li.

I kept my head down while I was completing the entry in the Register and filling in the marriage certificate. Denise called the bride Ken for most of the ceremony, but of course the legal vows required the full name to be repeated several times. Denise did her best, slowly and clearly pronouncing the name as "Waaan" (as in deficient in colour) but it was clearly meant to be pronounced "Wahn" and the couple duly responded so, which unsurprisingly brought forth some hilarity among the guests, especially on the groom's side.

The bride was clearly used to the boorish reaction to the reciting of her name and continued with dignity. I imagine her groom was also used to it, or had been warned that anything other than a straight face and loving looks would result in a violent reaction from his beloved. Once the legal vows were negotiated, the ceremony continued without further disruption, and I even remembered to say "Congratulations, Ken!" to the bride at the end of the ceremony.

On the subject of names, a colleague told me of a slight embarrassment she had recently. We have to ask how the couple and their witnesses sign their names, so that they can be transcribed accurately on the marriage certificate from often indecipherable scrawls in the Register. My colleague was interviewing Patrick Brain, and asked him "And how do you sign, P. Brain?"

Sometimes the county venues attract some famous people for ceremonies, both as guests and principals, and several Hollywood A-listers have been known to travel to Somerset for their nuptials. Several months ago I conducted the wedding of two actors in Orchardleigh House, and a colleague of the bride and groom was also in attendance to make a reading.

I rather imagined that I recognised him, but couldn't be sure, so I didn't give it much thought. I invited him forward at the appropriate time, and he stood in front of the guests to give his reading which, unsurprisingly, he delivered very well. When I later passed him on the way out of the marriage room, I said to him "That was well read!" and patted him on the shoulder. He gave me a broad grin.

It was only later that I discovered that I had patted the back of Oscar nominee Eddie Redmayne, and of course, shortly afterwards he won the Best Actor Oscar for his role as Professor Stephen Hawking in the film 'The Theory Of Everything'. I assume, because of his reaction, that he didn't object to my cheeky compliment, even if it was a bit like telling Lewis Hamilton that he was a good driver!

Guests are often asked to recite readings at wedding ceremonies, and these interludes are welcome as they give the registrar entering the details in the Register a little more time to complete the task, as well as allowing the conducting registrar a brief period away from centre stage. We hear a great many readings, some of which are a bit banal, but others – if well read, and possibly personal to the couple – definitely enhance a ceremony and are often met with appreciative applause from other guests.

I always include the name of the reader in my script to remind me to ask them to come to the front for the recitation, but on one occasion I missed giving the invitation and (with the couple's permission) asked the reader to come forward later in the ceremony.

Unfortunately the terms I used to make the invitation were probably not the most well-chosen. "Can I now ask Michelle to come forward to give her reading, and I apologise for not inserting her earlier...."

For some years now we have been conducting Civil Partnerships between same-sex couples. The procedure is slightly different, but the ceremony, with a few alterations, remains basically the same. At the end, instead of announcing "You are now husband and wife!" I would say to the couple, "You are now united in civil partnership!" (or since it became legal in the case of a marriage, if the couple want it, "You are now husband and husband!" or "...wife and wife!" Otherwise, quite simply, "You are now married!"), and a schedule would be signed certifying the legal event. I have conducted many such ceremonies and enjoyed them equally with all the others.

In fact I recall one civil partnership I conducted in Orchardleigh House with great pleasure. The couple concerned were two girls, both professional people in their 30s. I had been in communication with them beforehand via email, as they had wanted personalised vows and one or two other small changes, which I had permitted. Consequently I had come to know the pair, albeit from a distance. When I met them for interview before the ceremony, I saw that they were both good-looking intelligent women with a sense of humour, and we got along famously.

Neither girl had changed into their wedding clothes before the interview, so I left them to it, and took myself off to the marriage room to prepare for the ceremony. The guests filled the room, and the atmosphere was very happy and relaxed.

At the appropriate moment, I said, "Ladies and Gentlemen, please stand for the entrance of Susan and Diane!" I looked along the lengthy aisle as they entered the room, and the sight was breath-taking.

For some reason I'd expected one of the girls to be wearing a trouser suit or similar, but both wore beautiful white wedding dresses, and the effect was stunning. They processed together until they stood in front of me, holding hands and smiling. There were quite a few tears and nods of appreciation as they passed their guests, and the ceremony, I'm glad to say, went without a hitch. I still have a memory of the girls as they processed down the aisle towards me, and it was just such a delightful occasion.

Nowadays the Civil Partnership ceremony has more or less vanished from the scene as same-sex couples are permitted to marry each other. As far as I am concerned, it makes the ceremony simpler, because it mirrors almost exactly the opposite-sex ceremony, with obvious exceptions (both say to each other "lawful wedded husband" or "lawful wedded wife.") The Register and certificates are filled out in the same way, so any issues regarding schedules and other complications are avoided.

Before I joined the Registration Service, I assumed that ladies always knew how to dress, and were aware of what suited them best. However I have now come to the conclusion that my naive assumption is somewhat wide of the mark. Before I am pilloried by anybody, I acknowledge that this is just my opinion!

When attending a wedding, most people will dress in their best clothes with the intention of making a good impression at the event. However, in observing guests assembling for ceremonies, I have noticed that some fall far short of this intention, which presumably is to appear attractive and elegant.

As a mere man, I hesitate to be more specific about the height of a hemline, the width of a waist, or the distraction of a décolletage, but the last word which springs to mind in describing some of them is 'elegant'. Men can be equally unaware of what constitutes proper dress for a wedding, and a few seem to think it okay to come clothed in jeans and wearing trainers or flip-flops. We are fortunate, however, in that our wedding clothes are generally more uniform in character.

Having said all that, when the ladies get it right (as they still do in most cases) the result is very attractive, and is a major factor in making ceremonies memorable and happy events.

When we go to the bride's preparation room to interview her before the ceremony, we enter an arena sometimes crowded with bridesmaids and flower girls, all bedecked in wedding finery. I am privileged to get this preview, which is (I need hardly say) one of the bonuses of the day for a male registrar. When I say to the bride "You look amazing!" I usually mean it.

Needless to say, these observations only apply to ceremonies where standard dress is the order of the day. Themed ceremonies come into a different category, and on such occasions, of course, normal dress codes do not apply.

Just occasionally a bride can become a little demanding or obsessive about the details of her ceremony. Every effort is made to accommodate a couple's wishes, but we have to operate within the constraints applied to us by law.

As the emails fly backwards and forwards, a file can become quite thick as a bride asks indignantly why she cannot use the wedding vows composed especially for her by her great-aunt Beatrice, or insert favourite readings from the Bible, or indeed to get tied up in a kind of bondage activity.

I recall one such long-distance discussion, when a bride wanted a Biblical reading. (*"Oh, it's such a lovely passage about love, it doesn't mention God once, and I've always wanted it to be read at my wedding."*) The couple also wanted a hand-tying act to be part of the legal ceremony which again couldn't be allowed because of association with religious rituals.

This little problem was sorted out eventually by reducing the legal part of the marriage ceremony to a minimum. After brief introductions, the Declaration and Contractual vows were recited by the couple. Then the Register was signed and the certificate presented, after which the registrars departed, legal obligations completed.

Then another Celebrant, unconnected with the Registration Service, took over to complete the marriage (Bible and bondage included) to the couple's satisfaction – which was, of course, as much our objective as theirs.

Life goes on, and it is certain, even in my limited experience, that the act of matrimony is not going out of fashion. During the Spring and Summer months especially, we sometimes have four, five, or even six ceremonies on one day at a weekend, and perhaps two or three on a weekday. Unless the weddings are all taking place in a Registration Office, it means that we don't have a lot of time to drive from one venue to the next.

When driving to weddings, I am careful to select a route which avoids motorways. Motorways always bring with them the possibility of an inescapable holdup, either because of an accident or perhaps generally heavy traffic. I would not enjoy the stress of sitting in my stationary car knowing that the time of a wedding at which I was officiating was approaching, and not being able to do anything about it. Should such incidents happen on A roads at least you have the alternative of performing a U-turn and trying another route.

Of course, our journeys are managed so that there is sufficient time to get from ceremony to ceremony, and if every bride arrived on time there would be no problem. But if one of the brides (other than the last one) arrives late for her ceremony the knock-on effect can be quite a worry. Couples are advised during their early interviews that if timings are not met, they run the risk of the registrars having to depart without their ceremony having taken place. It is patently unfair if one bride's tardiness affects a later couple's arrangements.

I'm relieved to say that I have never left a venue with the couple still unmarried, but there have been a few close calls. Very rarely we have to shorten a ceremony by reducing the vows to the minimum, or omitting readings, so that we can get away quickly to the next venue. Sometimes the mere mention that this might happen is enough to concentrate the mind, and is sufficient to get a late bride down the aisle in short order.

You may be wondering now whether I have ever been involved in a ceremony where a bride or groom have changed their minds at the last minute, and fled. The short answer to that is 'no'. However, I am aware of that very thing happening at a ceremony in the south of the county two years ago, so the potential is always there.

For this reason, we do not begin to complete the entry in the Register until *after* the couple have correctly recited their Contractual vows, which in effect unites them in marriage.

On the vast majority of occasions it is obvious that the bride and groom are very happy, and no power on earth would prevent them from completing their marriage vows and becoming husband and wife. Then it is tempting, in order to save a little time, to fill the Register in early during the ceremony, but I have never done so.

It is not for Ceremony Officers to judge a relationship on the basis of a few minutes' acquaintance, but just occasionally I am aware of a kind of tension in the air, or an indefinable atmosphere which will certainly make me pause over the Register until the Contractual vows are safely recited.

The 'bondage' couple who insisted on our early exit from their ceremony robbed me, on that occasion, of the opportunity of giving my final "wise words" to them. I normally volunteer these just before they process back up the aisle as husband and wife.

I always ask the new husband to stand on his wife's right hand side, and I explain that it symbolises the crossing over and uniting of their two families, as well as keeping his sword arm free to protect his wife in the event of danger. (Some grooms nod sagely at this piece of information, as if it was normal practice to brandish a protective sword. And some say, "I'm left-handed!")

Then I would say to him, "I would like to point out that you are now on the right side of your wife. And if you take my advice, that's where you'll stay for the rest of your life." Very sensible advice, I always thought!

CONCLUSION

I set out to write a few stories about being a Ceremony Officer which I hoped were interesting, amusing, or just plain odd. I hadn't been writing for long, however, when I realised that most of the stories needed something extra – details about our policies and procedures had to be explained, or the scene needed to be set in some other way. In furnishing such details, which I hoped didn't reduce the generally light-hearted tone, the project became a little longer than I had originally intended.

Any of my colleagues could tell, if they chose, lots of stories connected with the job which would, no doubt, be more interesting or funnier than anything I have related. However, I have tried to keep these stories to those within my own experience, and just allowed three or four second-hand incidents to creep in – mostly for my own amusement and also because I thought they were worth recording.

Provided I can remain *compos mentis,* coherent, and upright, I hope to continue as a Ceremony Officer for many years to come. At any time incidents may occur which I will record in my notebook, so perhaps in due course I will take up my pen again to provide this book with a companion. If I do, it will be to salute my colleagues and the great marrying public who provide me with such an interesting and fascinating occupation, which makes it well worth while getting out of bed in the morning!

***

It occurs to me that some people who pick up this book may do so because they plan a civil marriage themselves. If that is the case, I thought it might be useful for them to have a brief summary of the legal requirements and practical procedures involved in organising a civil ceremony, and what might be expected of the Ceremony itself.

CIVIL WEDDINGS

GENERAL PROCEDURES

(The notes given below refer to ceremonies in England and Wales and do not include variations possible in other geographical areas or where foreign nationals are involved. For more detailed information, please check out Civil Marriages on the Web.)

(1) WHO CAN GET MARRIED?

In the UK, opposite-sex or same-sex couples can marry in a civil ceremony. All couples may marry if they are both 16 years or over and free to marry, e.g. if they are single, widowed or divorced (or dissolved in the case of civil partnership).

If either party is 16 or 17 years of age they cannot marry without parental consent. Both parents with parental responsibility must give consent.

Some relatives are not allowed to marry, and if they do the marriage is automatically void even if they do not know they are related.

(2) WHERE CAN A CIVIL MARRIAGE TAKE PLACE?

A civil marriage can take place in a Registration Office or other premises approved by the local authority, such as a hotel, stately home, or other appropriate building. The premises must be regularly open to members of the public, and be permanently built structures – approval will not be given for open air venues such as gardens, beaches or golf courses.

A list of approved premises can be obtained from the local Registration Office or found on the Web at www.gov.uk

(3) GIVING NOTICE

Both parties must give notice of marriage in their local Registration Office, whether or not they wish to marry in that district. The Superintendent Registrar or deputy then issues authority for the marriage and they may then marry in any Registration Office or approved premises in any district.

28 days' notice must be given to the Registration Office before the marriage can take place. Both parties must be resident for 7 days in England or Wales before notice is given. In the period between the notice of intention to marry and the ceremony, anyone with legal grounds for objecting to the marriage can do so. A notice must state where the marriage is to take place. Making a false statement is a criminal offence.

(4) PROCEDURE

Both parties will be asked for the following information when giving notice, and giving false information is a criminal offence:

(a) evidence of name and address

(b) evidence of date of birth

(c) if one party has been married before (or in a civil partnership) primary documentary evidence that the marriage or civil partnership has ended (e.g. Death Certificate or Decree Absolute)

(d) evidence of nationality.

A variety of documents can be used as evidence, but a passport, travel document or birth certificate is usually sufficient. Specific advice on what will be accepted can be obtained from the Register Office.

(5) CEREMONY

The marriage ceremony must be conducted by a person authorised to register marriages in the district.

The marriage ceremony will take approximately 15-20 minutes. The conducting Registrar (Superintendent Registrar) will make a short statement about marriage, and the ceremony may, if desired, include readings, songs, or other music.

It is not permitted to use religious words or music in the civil ceremony.

Each party is required to repeat a standard set of promises. These may not be changed, but can be added to, as long as the additions are not religious.

Rings are not obligatory but can be exchanged if desired.

After the ceremony, the marriage Register is checked as correct and then signed by both parties. Two witnesses (who must understand the language, and have the mental capacity to understand the nature of the ceremony) must also sign at the same time.

Registration staff are not allowed to act as witnesses. The Superintendent Registrar and the Registrar responsible for recording the marriage will also both sign the entry.

It is the beginning of a new life for the couple – congratulations! – but for you, the reader, it is…

THE END